THRY

Great Inventions

THE AIRPLANE

by Julie L. Sinclair

Consultant:
Ryan Lillie
Director of Education
Evergreen Aviation Museum
McMinnville, Oregon

Capstone *press*

Mankato, Minnesota

Fact Finders is published by Capstone Press
151 Good Counsel Drive, P.O. Box 669, Mankato, Minnesota 56002
http://www.capstone-press.com

Library of Congress Cataloging-in-Publication Data
Sinclair, Julie L.
    The airplane / Julie L. Sinclair.
    p. cm.—(Fact finders. Great inventions)
    Includes bibliographical references (p. 31) and index.
    Contents: A gift for two boys—Before the airplane—Inventors—How an airplane
works—The world begins to fly—Airplanes today.
    ISBN 0-7368-2213-5 (hardcover)
    1. Airplanes—History—Juvenile literature. [1. Airplanes—History.] I. Title. II. Series.
TL670.3 .S543 2004
529.133'34'09—dc21   2002156498

Editorial Credits
Roberta Schmidt, editor; Juliette Peters, series designer and illustrator; Enoch Peterson,
    illustrator; Alta Schaffer, photo researcher; Eric Kudalis, product planning editor

Photo Credits
Art Resource, NY/Scala, 11 (top)
Comstock, 17
Corbis, 20–21; Corbis/Museum of Flight, 26 (middle); James A. Sugar, 27 (left);
    Bettmann, 27 (middle)
Courtesy of Special Collections and Archives, Wright State University, 5 (both), 14, 15, 26 (left)
Creatas/Creatas/PictureQuest, cover
Digital Vision, 19, 27 (right)
Hulton/Archive Photos by Getty Images, 9, 11 (bottom), 12 (top), 13, 26 (right);
    Sean Sexton, 6–7
Index Stock Imagery/Debra Ashe, 24–25
Library of Congress, 12 (bottom)
North Wind Picture Archives, 8
PhotoDisc Inc., 1
Stock Montage Inc., 22–23

1 2 3 4 5 6 08 07 06 05 04 03

Table of Contents

Chapter 1

A Gift for Two Boys

One day in 1878, Milton Wright brought a gift home to his two youngest sons. Orville was 7 years old. Wilbur was 11. The gift was a toy helicopter. The helicopter was made of cork, bamboo, paper, and a rubber band.

Milton showed the boys how to make the helicopter fly. He wound the two propellers. He tossed the toy into the air. The helicopter flew. The boys were amazed. From that day forward, Wilbur and Orville wanted to build a flying machine. They hoped to ride in the machine and fly through the air.

Children played with toy helicopters for more than 100 years before full-sized aircraft were built.

Orville (left) and Wilbur (top) Wright dreamed of building and flying an airplane.

Chapter 2

Before the Airplane

Until the late 1800s, most people did not travel very far from their homes. Most people traveled by horse and wagon or by walking. But travel was changing. New machines were being built.

People were looking for new ways to travel. Engines powered by steam, gasoline, and electricity led to the invention of trains and automobiles. Trains and automobiles could travel longer distances. They made it easier for people to travel.

The first train rail in the United States was laid in 1828. By 1900, more than 190,000 miles (305,700 kilometers) of tracks crossed the country.

Before airplanes and automobiles, many people traveled by trains.

Automobiles and trains did not fix all traveling problems. Automobiles did not always make traveling easy. Early automobiles were uncomfortable. They did not have springs to make the ride smooth. They did not have heaters. Early automobiles also were unsafe and difficult to drive.

Early automobiles were not easy to drive.

Trains were not always a safe way to travel.

Trains had problems too. They did not go everywhere people wanted to go. Trains could travel only where there were railroad tracks. Trains also needed many people to care for the tracks. A train could run off its tracks if the tracks were damaged.

People wanted to make traveling easier and safer. Some inventors made better engines for automobiles. Others began to think about a new way of traveling. They dreamed of flying in the air like a bird.

Chapter 3

Inventors

Before and after the train and automobile, people tried to figure out how to fly. They wanted to build machines that would carry them safely through the air.

Leonardo da Vinci

One of the first people to design a flying machine was Leonardo da Vinci. Da Vinci lived in Italy in the late 1400s and early 1500s. He designed several machines with flapping wings. Da Vinci called his machines "ornithopters."

The Montgolfier Brothers

In 1783, Joseph-Michel and Jacques-Étienne Montgolfier built a large hot-air balloon. These French brothers wanted their balloon

Da Vinci drew many ornithopters.
The Montgolfier brothers tested their
first hot-air balloon in 1783 (below).

to carry people through the air.
But they were not sure if it was
safe for people. They put a sheep,
a duck, and a rooster in the
balloon's basket. These animals
were the first hot-air balloon
passengers. Later that year, people
used the balloon to fly over Paris.

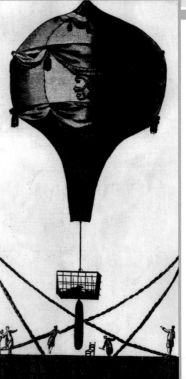

11

George Cayley

In 1804, Sir George Cayley built a special kite. It was set on a stick. It had a movable tail. This kite looked like a modern airplane.

Sir George Cayley sometimes is called the father of aviation.

Otto Lilienthal was a German engineer.

Otto Lilienthal

Almost 90 years later, Otto Lilienthal became interested in flying. He made his first flying vehicle in 1891. This hang glider had large wings and could soar through the air. Lilienthal later built other gliders. He learned a lot about flying by riding in his hang gliders.

The Wright Brothers

Wilbur and Orville Wright built the first flying craft that could be controlled while in the air. The brothers studied flying and mechanics for many years. They read about Lilienthal's hang gliders. They tested models. They built and flew large gliders.

The Wright brothers knew how to make a kite soar in the air. But they wanted to build a flying machine that powered itself.

Lilienthal flew often in his hang gliders. Most of his flights lasted 12 to 15 seconds and covered 985 feet (300 meters).

The Wright brothers flew in a hang glider before they built an airplane.

Wilbur and Orville worked hard to make an airplane. They designed and built a lightweight engine. They also made a propeller. In December 1903, their first airplane was ready to test. The *Flyer* was 21 feet (6.4 meters) long. Its wings were 40.5 feet (12.3 meters) wide. The *Flyer* weighed 605 pounds (274.4 kilograms) without a pilot.

On December 17, 1903, the Wright brothers took the *Flyer* to the sand dunes near Kitty Hawk, North Carolina. Orville sat in the pilot's seat. Wilbur ran along the side. Their plane flew 120 feet (37 meters) in 12 seconds. A self-powered machine had never before risen, flown in a straight line, and landed safely.

The Wright brothers flew in the *Flyer* for the first time on December 17, 1903.

Chapter 4

How an Airplane Works

The forces of flight are the ideas that help people understand how airplanes fly. These forces are thrust, lift, weight, and drag.

Thrust and Lift

Thrust moves a plane forward. Engines make thrust. Jet engines push the plane forward. Most propeller engines pull the plane forward. Thrust works with lift to make the airplane rise and fly.

The forces of flight help make even the simplest airplane fly.

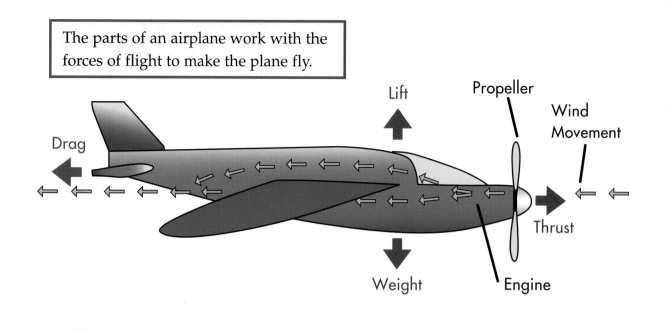

The parts of an airplane work with the forces of flight to make the plane fly.

Lift lets an airplane rise from the ground. A plane's wings are designed to make lift when the plane is moving. Lift happens when air moves faster on top of a wing than below it. This air movement takes pressure off the top of a wing. Lift lets the plane rise.

Weight and Drag

An airplane has to fight weight and drag to stay in the air. Weight makes the airplane fall toward the ground when the engine does not produce enough thrust. Drag also works against the airplane. Wind causes drag as it moves over the aircraft. It slows down the plane.

The Wright brothers studied and understood the forces of flight. They could build and fly an airplane because they knew these forces.

Concorde jets fly very fast. They have a lot of thrust and very little drag.

Chapter 5

The World Begins to Fly

Airplanes changed the world. Many countries realized that airplanes could be useful. In 1908, Wilbur and Orville Wright agreed to build planes for the U.S. Army. Many airplanes were used during World War I (1914–1918).

The airplane also changed travel and business. The first aircraft passenger service began in Florida in 1914. The plane took off and landed on water. It carried one passenger at a time. For $5, a person could cross Tampa Bay in 23 minutes. A boat needed two hours to make the same trip.

World War I was the first war in which airplanes were used widely.

In the early 1900s, many people were afraid to travel in an airplane. They thought airplanes were unsafe. During this time, few planes were built to carry passengers. Most planes were used to carry mail.

Charles Lindbergh changed the way people felt about flying. In 1927, he flew from New York City to Paris, France. Lindbergh was the first person to fly alone across the Atlantic Ocean. His flight made people excited about air travel. Many people started to fly in airplanes. Businesses started to build airplanes that could carry many people.

Charles Lindbergh flew across the
Atlantic Ocean in his airplane
called *Spirit of Saint Louis*.

Lindbergh's flight took 33.5 hours.
He flew without stopping for
3,600 miles (5,793 kilometers).

New Laws

Laws were set up to make
airplanes safe for travelers.
The Air Commerce Act of 1926
made many rules for air travel.
Planes had to be tested for
safety. Pilots also had to pass
tests before they could fly.

In 1967, the Federal
Aviation Administration
(FAA) was formed. The FAA
helps to make air travel safe.
One of the FAA's jobs is to
make sure planes fly safely.

Chapter 6

Airplanes Today

Inventors after the Wright brothers made airplanes larger, faster, and safer. More powerful engines let airplanes be built much bigger. These engines also made planes fly faster. People added controls to make airplanes safer. The instruments help pilots fly at night or in unsafe weather. Pressurized cabins and radar also help to make planes safer.

Passenger planes have changed over the years. The first modern passenger airplane was the Boeing 247.

Air travel is very popular today.

United Airlines introduced this airplane in 1933. The Boeing 247 traveled at 155 miles (249 kilometers) per hour. It could carry 10 passengers at a time. In 1935, American Airlines built the DC-3. This new airplane was faster, cheaper to fly, and safer for passengers. Because of these improvements, many more people became interested in air travel.

The United States has the largest flight system in the world. The United States has more than 18,000 airports and serves more than 30 million passengers each year.

Airplanes through the Years

Ford Trimotor
1926

Jenny JN-4
1916

Wright Flyer
1903

Airplanes are still changing.
Most of today's passenger airplanes
fly 550 miles (885 kilometers) per hour.
But people are building faster airplanes.
A Concorde jet can fly faster than
1,300 miles (2,090 kilometers) per hour.
Some military aircraft can fly more than
4,500 miles (7,242 kilometers) per hour.
As planes change, they become a more
common way of traveling.

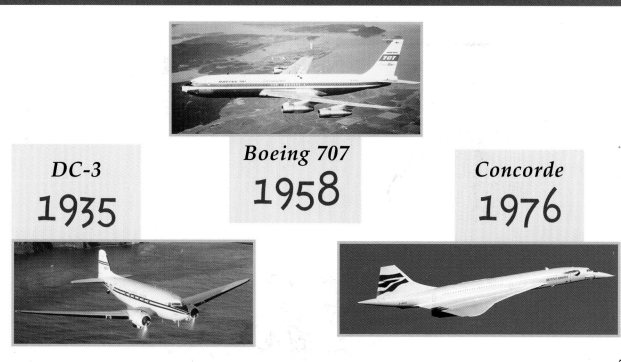

DC-3
1935

Boeing 707
1958

Concorde
1976

Fast Facts

- **Before airplanes,** most people traveled in wagons, in trains, or in automobiles.

- **Leonardo da Vinci** designed some of the first flying machines. He called his machines "ornithopters."

- **Otto Lilienthal** built his first hang glider in 1891. He learned about flying by riding in his hang gliders.

- In its first flight, the **Wright** *Flyer* flew 120 feet (37 meters). Later that day, the *Flyer* carried Wilbur 852 feet (260 meters) in 59 seconds.

- The **forces of flight** are thrust, lift, weight, and drag. These ideas help to explain how and why airplanes fly.

- **Charles Lindbergh** flew alone across the Atlantic Ocean in 1927.

- Most of today's **passenger airplanes** fly about 550 miles (885 kilometers) per hour.

Hands On:

Build a Kite

What You Need

newspaper	scissors	tape
measuring tape	string, at least 60 feet (18 meters)	
pencil	16-foot (5-meter) ribbon	

What You Do

1. Open a double page from the newspaper. Measure 7 inches (18 centimeters) from each corner. Mark the place with a dot. Draw lines to connect the dots. (See the red lines in diagram A.)
2. Cut off the corners, using your lines as a guide. The large shape will be your kite.
3. Tape around the edges and across the kite, as shown by the blue lines in diagram B.
4. Take two more double pages out of a newspaper. Roll them into very tight tubes.
5. Tape the tubes to the kite like the purple lines in diagram C.
6. Tape a 5-foot (1.5-meter) string to the top corners of the kite. Tape another 5-foot (1.5-meter) string to the bottom corners. (See the green lines in diagram D.)
7. Tie the ribbon to the bottom string.
8. Attach a very long piece of string to the top kite string. Hold this long string as you run and make your kite fly.

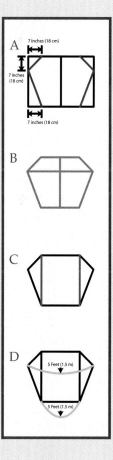

29

Glossary

aircraft (AIR-kraft)—a vehicle that can fly

aviation (ay-vee-AY-shuhn)—science of building and flying aircraft

design (di-ZINE)—to make a plan for how to build something

drag (DRAG)—the force that resists the motion of an object moving through the air

hang glider (HANG GLYE-dur)—an aircraft similar to a giant kite with a harness for a pilot hanging below it

lift (LIFT)—the force that lets an airplane rise from the ground and stay in the air

mechanics (muh–KAN–iks)—a part of science that deals with the way forces affect still or moving objects

thrust (THRUST)—the forward force produced by an engine

vehicle (VEE-uh-kuhl)—a machine that carries people and goods

Internet Sites

Do you want to find out more about the airplane?
Let FactHound, our fact-finding hound dog, do the research for you.

Here's how:
1) Visit *http://www.facthound.com*
2) Type in the **Book ID** number:
   0736822135
3) Click on **FETCH IT**.

FactHound will fetch Internet sites picked by our editors just for you!

Read More

Baysura, Kelly. *First Flight.* Flying Machines. Vero Beach, Fla.: Rourke, 2001.

Chant, Christopher. *Civil Aircraft.* The World's Greatest Aircraft. Philadelphia: Chelsea House, 2000.

Mitton, Tony. *Amazing Airplanes.* Amazing Machines. New York: Kingfisher, 2002.

Williams, Zachary. *How Do Airplanes Fly?* The Rosen Publishing Group's Reading Room Collection. New York: Rosen, 2002.

Index

THE   Y